PRAISE FOR BETSY L. JORDAN

"Being Betsy's client changed my outlook on life. There are self-help books, motivational movies, thoughtful quotes that give you a 'hmmm' moment, but there's nothing like the direct dynamic impact of Betsy's approach. There is such a thing as a mental shift, or altering your mind-set. I know this now, because Betsy Jordan helped me accomplish quite a shift with her unique coaching methods. Thank you Betsy for making all the difference in my world, I have a much better grasp on business and financial responsibility than ever before."

—Daniel Jones

"Betsy, brings a great energy and enthusiasm to her work. Creative, concise and fun to work with."

—Joseph C. D'Alessandro
Independent Media Production Professional

"I hired Betsy for executive coaching, and it was one of the best decisions I've made in a while. She revitalized key aspects of my career with her thoughtful and disciplined methodology. She is so intelligent and empathetic, yet she'll tell you when your full of sh*t when you need to hear it. I highly recommend her to turbo-charge your life."

—Chip Venters

CEO at BrowsePlay Interactive Video

"Betsy is an inspired leader with energy and passion to share her many gifts and talents. I recommend her without reservation."

—Denise Cline

Member at Law Offices of Denise Smith Cline, PLLC

"Betsy exemplifies the word *transformation* for that is what she offers all of her clients. Coaching with Betsy offers direct feedback and direct results!"

—Laura Gould

Owner/Coach at SwimLessonsRaleigh.com

"On a personal level, Betsy practices what she preaches. She never stops growing and learning."

—Will

"North Carolina's film industry was well served through Betsy's insight, hard work and commitment. Betsy championed projects that promoted the industry and was able to focus on the key issues that made a difference in how North Carolina competed against other states. She's a great ally to have on your team."

—Monty Hagler
President & CEO, RLF Communications

"Betsy Jordan is a visionary who can see beyond the routine tasks of the day. She has a gift for marketing and putting together resources to accomplish her goals. Betsy is a leader and can influence others with her keen insight, clear communication style and engaging personality."

—Bob Jamieson
Living Seaside Realty Group

"I was well served through Betsy's insight, hard work and commitment. She's a great ally to have on your team."

—Monty Hagler

"Betsy is a results oriented person, one you will be glad to have had the pleasure to meet, and delighted she's always working in your best interests."

—Carol Spiller, CMB

"Betsy Jordan has a keen insight into helping people achieve their life goals. She has an uncanny knack for breaking down barriers that may be creating obstacles for people that they cannot see for themselves: a frequent life-staller; spending time with Betsy is like drinking from a cold fountain on an incredibly hot day; you always want to come back for more! Take making a change in your life seriously and give Betsy a call; you won't be sorry!"

—Anna Watson Blair
Infusion Therapy Nurse at UNC-Hospitals

"Betsy is bright and highly intuitive. Her assistance with me at a critical point in my life's journey was instrumental in helping me in many areas, both professional and personal. Anyone hiring her will be rewarded many times over."

—Joe Christian

Performance Coach

"Betsy is an amazing business woman with dead-on intuition and a plethora of skills and experiences to draw from. I recommend her without reservation."

—Trish Thomas

CEO at Atomic20

"Betsy is a seasoned professional who brings her high energy level and professionalism to everything she does. Having her work with you and your company is a great investment."

—Teena Anderson

Non-Profit Organization Management Professional

INTER-DIMENSION

WITH

COMPANION JOURNAL

BOOKS BY BETSY L. JORDAN

Seven Absolute Keys to Create Anything:!

Coach! Seven Keys for the Beginning Coach

Key 1, Oneness, with Companion Journal

Key 2, Inter-Dimension, with Companion Journal

Key 3, Movement, with Companion Journal

Key 4, Paradox, with Companion Journal

Key 5, Exchange, with Companion Journal

Key 6, Personal Power, with Companion Journal

Key 7, Yin/Yang, with Companion Journal

BullsEye!

The Seven Tactics To Hit The Bull's Eye In Your Business

Film Industry Professional's Edition

Book One: Connect!

Book Two: See!

Book Three: Act!

Book Four: Experience!

Book Five: Expand!

Book Six: Power Up!

Book Seven: Launch!

KEY 2

INTER-DIMENSION

WITH

COMPANION JOURNAL

BY BETSY L. JORDAN

Dedicated to my remarkable *mentors*.

They had their work cut out for them!

"Your time is limited, so don't waste it living someone else's life. Don't be trapped by dogma, which is living with the results of other people's thinking. Don't let the noise of others' opinions drown out your own inner voice. And most important, have the courage to follow your heart and intuition."

—Steve Jobs

CONTENTS

AUTHOR'S NOTE

Many coaches will understand the principles covered herein automatically. My desire is that coaches use these universal principles of creativity and develop a language to use in their practices, troubleshooting as they go along. For example, the client who understands "oneness" and networks easily, may need work in the area of "personal power" if they are networking for approval. Or, a client who has no trouble imagining their future (inter-dimension) who yet won't get up off of the sofa needs work in the area of "movement." Let the seven keys be your framework.

Betsy Jordan

INTER-DIMENSION,
THE SECOND KEY

"Enlightened leadership is spiritual if we understand spirituality not as some kind of religious dogma or ideology but as the domain of awareness where we experience values like truth, goodness, beauty, love and compassion, and also intuition, creativity, insight and focused attention."

—Deepak Chopra

INTRODUCTION

The Difference

How many relationships, jobs, classes, experiences, great ideas, and coaching clients—even, have you experienced in your life? If we are alike in any way, you and I, it's probably safe to assume that we have both had great experiences and achievements, and have both had our share of failures and mishaps, too. In fact there is a lot that ten different jobs, three different careers, moving around the United States, one child, two stepsons, and two marriages will teach you, but the real difference came when I made a few simple changes in my life:

Focus and application.

As a positive, interested human being, I read, watched, listened, attended, and really did absorb a great deal of good information. Still, failure and success seemed somehow determined unconsciously and haphazardly until I focused on what were emerging as key principals and made very sure I applied what seemed true enough to possibly be universal. *Keys* started to rise to the top of my experiences when I employed attentive focus with application. Thrilling—simply thrilling. And today I get to share what I have learned with you, because my life after that point of discovery has been different, to say the least.

Seven *keys* unlock those doors you might have fought to get to, only to find them locked—the few keys that open to your own treasure trove of manifested dreams. These are the few really important doors in life, doors that lead to your own creativity and ability. What others call "luck" is explained in these pages.

But you've heard that before, right? In fact the bookstores are full of books making that very same claim, so what's the difference? Why read this book and others in my series? Simple. *You.* Let's be honest, there is a glut of information—good information—out there and probably even in your own library or on your own Kindle, so why read more? Well, the fact that you *are* reading more tells me two things: for all the good advice you've already found you want more which means you likely have *still* not completely found the right answers for *you*, and second, I believe most advisors do not allow into their equations the most important variable, which is, as I've said, *you.*

I want you to take the Seven Keys and make them yours, to understand these Seven Keys and apply them in *your own* way and to your unique situations and relationships. I want you to find these keys so natural after a period of focus and application that they become second nature, and what others see as a "knack" or "luck" seem to follow you wherever you go. I want you to have your own Midas touch as a result of your new acquaintance with *the Seven Keys*.

And there are seven. Some say this is the number of the mystic and indeed, throughout the ages seven has had a special place in the world. God created the heavens and the Earth in seven days. The Greek God Hermes is credited with scribing an ancient text with seven natural laws. Life itself is often described as having a seven-year cycle (or a seven-year itch). And after all of my own research and observation, the number seven simply seems to present itself universally, and in profound and powerful ways. So, seven it is.

And I now know there is *power* and an ability to *consciously create* what I really want, what you really want. Things are different now, thanks to that *knowledge*. And it did transition from a *belief* to a *knowledge* after consistently getting results with the seven keys. And when I consider sharing this knowledge it strikes me that I have plenty in my own life I wish I had *not* created, but to shy away from these things, you'll see, only pulls us back into the trap that beleaguers

5

most people, the belief that we *cannot* create our own thoughts, that we cannot manifest our own beauty and even our own greatness. In fact, even today when I end up with something that I am not consciously creating, I know that I get to learn from it, but I also know I get to move on from there to consciously change my own thoughts in order to create something different, something desirable. I know that there is power and the ability to consciously create what I really want, when I am fully accountable for it all.

You choose: which is more empowering, when you blame circumstances or people around you for anything non-ideal in your life *or* knowing that you are responsible for all of your life *and can therefore change it?* Important choice to make. And your life is happening *now and you are in it*—this is not a "waiting room" by any means. Too many valuable people still see it that way.

In fact the former choice is actually the more practical one, and before you take any knowledge and consider it, it should, after all, be practical. All my roads have led me here. I have studied with various people, as mentioned I've read, listened, watched, attended, and I've experimented with my own life. I have things in my own background you would be very able to relate to: failures and successes. There are enough of the first that would make us empathetic friends, and plenty of the second that would establish my credibility to lead on this issue, to capture your imagination for self- and world-improvement, just as the discovery of these seven keys has captured mine.

Anyone can learn these seven keys, either for oneself or as a philosophy with which to help others. We all create our worlds subconsciously everyday anyway, why not take charge of that facility? This book is an attempt to give you the tools that I now apply in my own life and my own practice, and these tools can now be shortcuts for you and your own clients!

But it's not magic, either. Learning to be aware takes practice.

Although some very important parts of the process cannot be "seen," they are as real as those parts that you can see. In fact, the world of the "unseen" is arguably more important than the world of the "seen," and this will become more clear as we move forward. With each key that we explain you (and your clients) will be given a chance to work with it, to do exercises which give you a practical experience of the key. I have found—through my own experience and through information that frankly, has simply come through me—that each key has a corresponding chakra, or area in the energetic body to which it corresponds. The chakra system is an energetic system which is explained through Vedic science, and which the Hindu religion has located just outside of the body but close to very specific areas of connection. You can use these areas of the body as touch points to remember the Seven Keys. Other than that, please see the appendix on the chakras at the back of this book and visit texts on the chakra system to understand more about that connection. My intention here is to keep things simple.

The way that I believe creativity comes through most quickly is from the 7th chakra down. In other words, I believe creativity can best be explained from the spiritual plane through manifestation, from the intellectual to the material, and from head to toe. You have a thought, the thought becomes manifest after action is taken.

Yet you do not have to believe this to benefit from the exercises or the information. My intention is to give you the tools to build a foundation for creating the life you dream of, with confidence that you are in tune with the natural elements of the universe, and to do so as quickly as possible.

I wish you all you have ever dreamed of.

And once you've assembled your own *Seven Keys* with focus and application, how will your life be different? How will your coaching practice change? And who will you help?

"Mathematics as an expression of the human mind reflects the active will, the contemplative reason, and the desire for aesthetic perfection. Its basic elements are logic and intuition, analysis and construction, generality and individuality."

—Richard Courant

INTER-DIMENSION

Big and small, everything is made of the same *stuff,* if organized in different ways and at various densities. That's why we can study and learn about the world in terms of *microcosms* and in terms of *macrocosms.* And in everything there is movement, too. And if you step back from this you'll see that we—all of us—are always operating simultaneously on different levels.

So close your eyes for a moment and let's explore a little inter-dimensionality. First, imagine yourself as you are now, then imagine yourself as you were as a small child. Open your eyes and realize that there is always some part of you that is *aware* of *you.* You are always watching yourself, in some sense, and you are still as you are now, still as you were. And just that simply, you have just experienced and inter-dimensionality about yourself, experienced yourself in different dimension.

11

Each of us has an "M-O," or a *modus operandi,* and it may be easier to see than you might at first think. They say a cluttered desk equals a cluttered mind, a violent driver, moves violently through life in other ways, and so on. We have certain ways of approaching things that apply whether it's to our friends, our relationships, our family, ourselves, our work, and the rest of life.

How we do *anything* is just how we do *everything.*

As we sow, so shall we reap.

As the big world, so is the small world.

And our very thoughts are what become things and actions in the real world.

Inter-dimensionality.

We are constantly operating in different dimensions, and at different levels. I know I have proven this to myself many times over. So what about you?

Michael Roach, in his great book, *The Diamond Cutter,* lays out certain *cures* for things we might encounter in the world of business. He also asserts that affirmations can and do heal the body. I suggest this is very true. When we think we influence our emotions, and a chain reaction ensues. It can actually be followed until we see effects on our very cells. And in turn we create effects in the world. We think , we react, we take action, and there are *ripples* that emanate from all of this. Our thoughts effect the entire world.

Cause and effect.

Knowing that we are inter-dimensional creatures can add tremendous value to whatever it is that we are about. Let's say, for example, that I am acting in a role and I want to get myself "out of the way," as actors will often say. I don't want *my* habits to be my character's habits. First of all, you have to notice who you are, notice what you are. The person that I am on the other side of that lens in that camera right now may not be the person that's in alignment with that character. So I take a look at who it is that I am, I look at my hand gestures, my movements, my this and that, and I consider, "Okay, if I'm going to be this character maybe they have a nervous laugh, maybe they're laughing all the time." So I add that, but I add it my way. And I can layer that nervous laughter.

It's the same thing as when you are getting a product to market, when you are creating something that is tangible. Let's say it's a camera, for instance. Well, you're going to do your best to imagine what the person who will be using this camera, your end user, will be wanting. It's always helpful to be able to empathize, to stand in the other person's shoes, and that's what I mean by inter-dimension. We are very multi-faceted beings.

So in standing in someone else's shoes, in standing in your customer's shoes, if you're making a transition out of

13

one relationship and into another, in standing in another's shoes and being inter-dimensional that way, you can create decisions that really enrich your life.

I invite you to do just that.

"Man is a microcosm, or a little world, because he is an extract from all the stars and planets of the whole firmament, from the earth and the elements; and so he is their quintessence."

—Paracelsus

INTUITION

All too often intuition is pooh-poohed and frowned on in business and other arenas, yet secretly okay for the person at the top. Perhaps the age of science ushered in a distaste for trusting your gut, hunches, inclinations, even the "feminine mystique." But as we delve into intuition and inter-dimension, these things, looked upon as senses, move to front and center.

In fact it's been shown that we all have an electromagnetic field around us. When the weather is just right, you can get little shocks from touching things, in fact. Some people see auras. I myself see *imprints*. Someone can enter the room, leave, and I will see the imprint they leave behind. And these fields—your aura, your electromagnetic field—both attract and repel people. In fact they are more powerful at attraction and repelling than even body language.

That's because these are universal forces. Auras can be photographed, and both fields can be experienced by many.

In 1992 I dreamed of my two-year-old daughter—a "future" daughter, for she was not yet born—and the dream included her appearance, her manner, and so on. In 1993. I met the man that would become her biological father, and he might have known it because I made it clear that if he wanted us to be together we were going to have a child! and in 1995 she was finally born. By 1997, my two-year-old daughter *looked and acted* just as she had in my dream, five years earlier.

My friend and editor has had the *same* experience, seeing his daughter, hair, freckles and all, even before his wife became pregnant.

We *do* manifest our dreams.

Or perhaps we dream about what we intend to manifest. Either way, it's not necessarily true that whatever we dream we manifest, but is clear that what we *intend,* what we become very clear about, can become created in the physical world— in the "real" world.

We create.

Sometimes we create unknowingly, as when we react. Sometimes it's pleasant and sometimes not. For example, should we meet someone, fall in love, marry, have children (or step-children), we might not have pre-envisioned but at a certain point we certainly develop such a vision!

We need only recognize that we are more than our physical, visible bodies, in fact, it would probably blow your mind to realize just how inter-dimensional we really are, and in this case, I want your mind to be blown!

See, you can *change* how you react to thoughts and happenings; you can change how you react to memories. This of course changes your resulting actions and the ripples you place upon the world. This leads to different *results. And therefore, you can actually change your past in the sense that you bring different things then into the future, and this happens simultaneously on so many different levels.*

Applying this second key of Inter-Dimension can support you in removing those filters which limit you. It can propel you forward with new reactions and new actions. It can change your *results* in your life and your career, in your relationships as well.

"In some sense man is a microcosm of the universe; therefore what man is, is a clue to the universe. We are enfolded in the universe."

—David Bohm

RESULTS

A h, one of my favorite words. I like results. I like results so much that sometimes we are attached. I *am* my results. I get totally addicted to them. And then, "Oh boy, there's my trouble."

Results are a way to see where you are, to determine how far you have to go, to see what's working, and what is missing. They point me inward to see what I get to do, ways I get to me in my business which lead me to my bull's-eye.

When you can see your results as a road map, you can turn right or left to stay on track. When you are attached to the results, lamenting that you aren't where you should be or holding on too tightly to the wheel, its wearing and takes longer to get there!

"My passion for gardening may strike some as selfish, or merely an act of resignation in the face of overwhelming problems that beset the world. It is neither. I have found that each garden is just what Voltaire proposed in *Candide*: a microcosm of a just and beautiful society."

—Andrew Weil

SYNESTHESIA

Let's take *synesthesia* as an example of inter-dimension. What the word means is an "intermingling of the senses," or several things happening at the same time on different levels. It's "cross-sensory" experience and explains why, in our culture, we have expressions like "loud clothing" or we refer to D.H. Lawrence's writing as "purple." The stimulation of one sense triggers others as well. A sight can come packaged with sound, tactile, smell, and so on. Some neurologists believe that this is the result of lingering connections, normally severed, in the brain.

And some are making effective and creative use of this phenomenon. A car engineer in Germany sees shapes and colors when he touches parts of a car. Ford Motor Company takes his advices on the design of steering wheels, door handles, and more. People who can harness synesthesia can use it.

Creativity and innovation are two large areas enhanced by this *ability*. And while the phenomenon has been known for millennia, we are beginning in a larger way to harness what can be done.

What can *you* do, by tapping into your own sense of inter-dimension? I'm sure you have ideas by now or can imagine a few. And when we get to the exercises in this book, imagine being rooted in the first key of Oneness, then releasing your own awareness of Inter-Dimension.

Enjoy the results!

"Faith is a passionate intuition."

—William Wordsworth

KEEPING VISION ALIVE

As coaches who have worked with clients to identify their vision of the future many of us have discovered that sometimes people do not see with their mind's eye readily. In fact, some people have trouble having a vision of the future at all. They may be more experiential in their learning style, or auditory in their learning style. So it is helpful when you think about inter-dimension to pull in some of these other senses when you are asking someone to visualize their futures.

With someone who has a more dominant auditory faculty for example, you might ask questions like:

"What are people saying to you ten years from now?"

"What are you feeling after achieving this?"

"What are you feeling against your skin?"

"What clothing are you wearing?"

And so on.

This puts them in touch with the fourth chakra as well, the Key of Paradox. It is also is the fourth tactic in *BullsEye!* before you actually manifest.

One thing that had me confused when I began to coach is how easily people will lose their vision and lose their way when they come up against something that may be considered a challenge or an obstacle. As clear as you can get them to be about the vision for their life, for their work, it's important to keep reinvesting in that vision every day in many different ways. It's important to separate these keys in terms of executing them. And try synthesizing them as you go along down the seven keys.

Ask them always to describe in great detail what they are seeing as they are visualizing their ideal work-life or ideal lifestyle. That will add fuel to their activities now and will also get them beyond any fear they may have.

We know that focusing on something, putting your attention on something, causes it to happen faster and the other ancillary worries fade away.

"You have to leave the city of your comfort and go into the wilderness of your intuition. What you'll discover will be wonderful. What you'll discover is yourself."

—Alan Alda

INTER-DIMENSIONAL
DECISIONS

Rich decisions in our creative work happen when we consider the Key of Inter-Dimension. Knowing that we are inter-dimensional creatures adds so much value. Let's say I'm acting in a role and I want to get out of the way. In other words, I want my habits to be "turned down" so that the person that is perceived through the camera right now is in alignment with that character I wish to be. Maybe this character has a nervous laugh, for example, so you layer it onto that character but you make it your own.

It's the same thing as when you are getting ready to market a product. You want to do your best to imagine what the person, the end user of the camera, is all about. It's always helpful to have empathy and to be able to visualize walking in their shoes.

And making a transition out of one relationship and into another, it's critical to see the other person as inter-dimensional as well.

I invite you to see yourself as making decisions inter-dimensionally.

CONCLUSION

The Seven Keys are here for you, unearthed and available to you. I can show and describe them but only you can pick them up and approach your goals and dreams with them, ready to unlock the barriers so many others find impassable. It's my hope that you *try* them after understanding them, that you perfect their use, that you use this and all books on the subject to improve first your own life and then the lives of your clients. I hope they become second nature to you. All of us can benefit massively from a knowledge of the Seven Keys and if we coach others they become even more important, so that we and our clients can create what we want, right where we are. We no longer need to wonder, be frustrated, or seek the approval of others or even the environment.

Armed with this book series you can make a difference. These books are not the fastest route, however, to learning the Seven Keys and their application. That comes from a live event, where through your own commitment and focus, your results will be fast and powerful. See the back of this book to discover how you can attend a seminar or webinar, how you can become certified in the training of others in The Seven Keys, and how you too can benefit from receiving coaching as well as from delivering it. It might be easier than you think to get connected, but even were it not, what would it be worth to train in tapping into your own massive creativity? What about your clients?

And never think that seeking improvement suggests you lack in any way. You have all you need right now, right where you are. The trick is getting to it. We are each whole and complete beings, with untapped potential and an opportunity for actualization. We can each make our dreams come true. Holding a client, friend, or loved one to a higher standard is also not to make less of someone, but more, especially if they themselves desire it. Many don't seem to desire it simply because they are unaware or do not believe it's possible. We know better.

You are uniquely you, and the only one. And you are complete. You only need to unlock what lies inside.

I hope that you take these keys and unlocking your barriers, live the life I believe you deserve. I hope you find abundance in all you seek in whatever arenas you find you love, and in whatever form this may be. I hope you find this all to be an incredible adventure, because it is just that—the adventure of *you*. And you have gifts for the world, that the world needs and needs badly.

Give a man a fish and he eats for perhaps a day, but teach him to fish and he can feed himself, his family, his friends and community as long as there are fish. And when we create abundance for those around us we seem to have it ourselves. When we see strength, intelligence, goodness in others and grant them as much we have effectively created those things or at least planted the seeds of those things. The opposite is, well, the opposite. *Pity,* for example. When given or received leads to weakness and a weakened relationship as well. Any immediate gratification is short lived, of course. In fact taken to an extreme, this is the road to resentment! Giving when you lack leads only to more lack if you are giving only with the intention of feeling better or bigger yourself. Giving from a place of abundance however, creates it for everyone.

Giving with the idea of improving someone else's life *while also* improving your own is about one of life's greatest answers. The greatest partnerships—whether it's a husband and wife, business partners, or even a coach and client—are created by two wholly independent people who choose to be together because they can and want to be together. Partnerships created out of dependency leave one partner

35

stronger than the other. They spiral downward as they are based on contraction, lack, and fear.

Yet we are, each of us, whole and complete beings.

And there is nothing broken about you or your clients, only untapped, locked away, in ways unique to each client. In fact we only do maintenance and development here, the repair shop is somewhere else. And part of that development is first recognizing, which is easy to do, the magnificence in each person. All you need to do is look.

May you celebrate your magnificence and that of each client through a life of passionate work and sound knowledge, may you and those you help then bring your own special gifts to the world!

Grounded in the Key of Oneness;

Understanding the influence of the Key of Inter-
Dimension;

You know your dreams are manifest *before* you see
them!

"There is no logical way to the discovery of these elemental laws. There is only the way of intuition, which is helped by a feeling for the order lying behind the appearance."

—Albert Einstein

THE 7 KEYS

TO CREATING THE LIFE YOU HAVE DREAMED OF!

Key #1, Oneness

Key #2, Inter-Dimension

Key #3, Movement

Key #4, Paradox

Key #5, Exchange

Key #6, Personal Power

Key #7, Yin~Yang

COMPANION JOURNAL

"The more you trust your intuition, the more empowered you become, the stronger you become, and the happier you become."

—Gisele Bundchen

Exercise ~ The Child in You

1. Take a minute and close your eyes.

2. Imagine yourself as a small child. Do you see that in your mind's eye?

3. Close your eyes and imagine that you are looking at yourself. Can you see you?

4. Open your eyes. Write about your experience.

Exercise ~ The Unseen

1. Gather a group of people.

2. Instruct everyone to put a personal item in a paper bag, telling no one what the item is.

3. Each person in the room chooses an object that they do not recognize.

4. Each person one by one describes the owner of the object. Continue until all object owners have been described. Don't reveal the owner until the exercise is completed.

5. Each owner, goes round the room and acknowledges accuracies in the description.

6. Notice the unseen.

Exercise ~ Sub-Personalities

1.   Stand in a room by yourself.

2. Relax your body by lightly stretching and taking a few deep breaths.

3. Identify several sub-personalities or archetypes that represent different facets of you. For example, I have a general, a little boy on the playground, Aphrodite, sad shy sally.

4. Now "place" those personalities in their own "spot" in the room.

5. As you step into each of those spots, take on the persona of that personality.

6.   As you take on each sub-personality persona, either write or record from that "voice" your ideal vision for your life.

7. When you have completed this, go back to the integrated you. How did your vision change?

8.   Do you see a way to incorporate all views into one big juicy vision?

9.   How does this represent inter-dimension?

Exercise ~ Hide an Object

This next step I think is truly cool:

1. With an attitude of non-judgment (oneness), ask
    someone—a friend, a child, a neighbor—to hide an
    object.

2. Once they hide that object, sit with them.

3. Close your eyes and imagine that you are the object. Note your impressions.

4. Then locate the object and see how your impressions match with the location from the "object's" point of view.

5. Take turns.

6. Repeat this often until you get better and better at it. This helps you visualize and manifest your visions quicker. It's also fun!

Exercise ~ Unlocking with The Keys

The key of oneness explains the idea that if we are arguing with someone in this part of the world, this leaves a mark on someone else in another place. It's not a chain reaction or anything as clearly direct, yet it has an effect just the same. It explains why Mother Teresa would say, "You will not see me at an anti-war rally. If you have a peace rally, please invite me." She understood oneness, as well as polarity or paradox and expansion versus contraction. She knew we are all connected, she knew to focus on the thing that is the highest and best good to get the results she wanted, and she also knew that what she placed her attention on would expand.

All of the keys overlap. The process of creativity is integrated and happens regardless of what we think about it. We are always breathing, our blood is always pumping. We create new cells in our body every second. With every thought that we think; we are creating. At the level of thought and emotion, we can affect things in the world that we do not see.

In the following exercise, when we tested it, we found that it was effective in demonstrating that we can affect others simply by our thoughts and feelings. I was surprised when we discovered that the person with their eyes closed would often respond or react and not even be aware of their reactions! I see this exercise now as a way to illustrate the key of exchange, the key of oneness, the key of inter-dimension, the key of paradox, the key of personal power on a subtle level. However, I believe it applies best to the key of movement as it clearly shows we affect others by our own thoughts, and that once we accept that we do, we can affect everything around us by never even saying a word.

1. Put one person in the front of the room with their eyes closed or blindfolded.

2. You or someone else act as facilitator, and you whisper to other participants a word such as joy, sexiness, frustration, etc.

3. The participants go up one by one and without saying a word, they do their best to generate the word that they are given in the person who has their eyes closed.

4. After a short while ask the person at the front of the room to open his or her eyes or remove the blindfold, and talk about their thoughts during the exercise.

"Spirituality can release blocks, lead you to ideas, and make your life artful. Sometimes when we pray for guidance, we're guided in unexpected directions. We may want a lofty answer and we get the intuition to clean our bedroom. It can seem so humble and picky and that you don't necessarily think of it spiritual guidance."

—Julia Cameron

ABOUT BETSY JORDAN

Betsy Jordan holds a PhD in Experiential Training through the Legacy Center, and Direct Impact. Further training in leadership development and coaching helped her focus on how we can effectively cause transformation in our lives and businesses. "The river that runs through my career is the exciting world of human development." She has studied with Deepak Chopra, MD., becoming one of the first mind/body educators in the country. "Studying with Deepak helped me to see the science behind thoughts causing reactions in our bodies". That degree opened doors for her work in quality customer service with major corporations in hospital supplies and banking industries. Betsy has a BS in Business Administration from the University of North Carolina at Chapel Hill.

Betsy's life experiences have encompasses the creative community, the corporate world and the unique challenges of entrepreneurship. Whatever challenges you face, she is the coach who can relate, resolve problems, and turbo-charge your results. Her pioneering work on creativity is published in her book, *Seven Absolute Keys to Create Anything!* as well as a number of forthcoming publications. Please watch for new titles and materials as they are released.

START TODAY!

THE TIME TO BEGIN your perfecting of the seven keys is *right now*. Your full life of passion, your independence from waiting on politicians to gain their senses or the film industry to seek you out is at hand.

www.BullsEyeCoach.com

SEMINARS & WEBINARS

FIND OUT ABOUT UPCOMING seminars and webinars by visiting this website:

www.BullsEyeCoach.com

COACHING

AND FOR YOUR QUICKEST route to perfecting the seven tactics and to experience The BullsEyeCoaching™ process (which includes the seven tactics), *contact me today.* I look forward to meeting you and hearing your ideas!

info@BullsEyeCoach.com

ACKNOWLEDGEMENTS

THIS IS A WORK about life. I could say that I thank everyone who ever touched my life directly and indirectly for all of you have been teachers, and I mean that sincerely. In this way, you all have contributed to the writing of this book.

To my mentors, all of you: Ray, Michael, Lori, Rob, James, Sam. Let me leave a special notice to my mentor, Deepak Chopra, whose groundbreaking work in the psycho-physiological origins of disease taught me so much about how the mind and the body are related. Through Carolyn Myss in her *Anatomy of the Spirit* I recognize that even in irreverence there is still reverence.

Thanks to Louise Hay whose bravery and generosity has helped so many people overcome ailments in the body. To my mentors at the legacy center, Robb and Lori in particular, I thank you so much for the true stand you are in the world for so many people. For my mentor Michael Strasner who sees the humor in all things and always finds that balance.

To my former husbands both of whom taught me the extraordinary strength and power of faith. To the great loves of my life who are numerous and so I would rather they know who they are and be grateful that we had that love. Once I choose to love someone, I *always* do, even if we disagree.

Sean Roach, I wouldn't have ever thought about writing these books if not for your brilliance and direction. And Rodney Miles, thank you so much for your contribution above expectations and execution of this series. I look forward to many, many years with this team of amazing people.

To the boys of my heart, Kyle and Taylor, who taught me that parenting had nothing to do with being of the same genetic make-up. And finally, to my sensitive and brilliant daughter who shows me every day what a miracle life is.

THE CHAKRAS

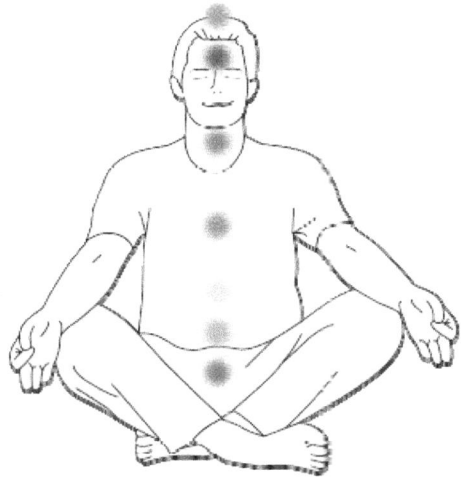

Figure 1: The seven chakras and their locations in the body.

The word "chakra" comes from a Sanskrit word meaning "wheel," (or "spinning point of light) and in some religions of India are considered points of energy and part of the intangible body that influences the physical body. Energy channels through these points. While there are believed to be many and various *nodes* or chakras throughout our bodies, these are the seven most important.

According to Caroline Myss in her book *Anatomy of the Spirit*, all of our thoughts and experiences are filtered through these chakras which function in part as databases, and are associated with our physical and mental selves as well as certain colors.

Some associate the chakras with specific nerve centers and glandular functions, and each is associated with various energies, all of which can be understood and placed into harmony.

THE 7 KEYS

TO CREATING THE LIFE YOU HAVE DREAMED OF!

Key #1, Oneness

Key #2, Inter-Dimension

Key #3, Movement

Key #4, Paradox

Key #5, Exchange

Key #6, Personal Power

Key #7, Yin~Yang

7 KEYS SUMMARIES

Key 1, Oneness

Oneness, all, we are the same stuff, we affect and are affected by each other, remove judgment of self and others.

Located above the head. 7th Chakra.

Key 2, Inter-Dimension

Inter-dimension, all levels, all of the time, awareness at the level of "before language," thoughts become things, know what you "know."

Located between the eyes (third eye). 6th Chakra.

Key 3, Movement

Movement, constant motion even at subtle levels... everything moving, language is the great creator, in the beginning was the Word, Thumper in the movie *Bambi* was correct: "If you can't say somethin' nice, don't say nothin' at all." Even subtler, if you can't "think "anything nice, then don't think anything at all, or at the very least, get outta the room!

Located at the throat (voice box). 5th Chakra.

Key 4, Paradox

Paradox, in every challenge lies the seed of its solution. Opposites exist. Polarity. Focus on positive and dismiss all lack and thoughts of lack. Want lots of goodies in your life, warm and fuzzies? Create it for others. Want love? Create it in every interaction. What we focus on expands. Decide with the heart.

Located above the heart. 4th Chakra.

Key 5, Exchange

Exchange, the Universe (God) rewards expansive plans. Giving and receiving both are expansive actions. Taking is a contracting energy—it interrupts expansion and leads to contraction. Give what you most want in a manner that creates this for others. Associated with gut feeling or solar plexus.

Located above the solar plexus. 3rd Chakra.

Key 6, Personal Power

Personal power, we are all whole and complete, no matter what our size and shape, number of fingers and toes, we can never give our power away. In our most complete and powerful understanding of ourselves, we understand the laws of cause and effect. We are able to respond to it all. Owning our power means that we have released "victim" consciousness. From the place of personal strength, ownership of it all, we can create something different. There is nothing more powerful than *you!*

Located above the abdomen. 2nd Chakra.

Key 7, Yin/Yang

Male/female, there lies within us the feminine and masculine principles and properties of creativity. Feminine is nurturing, gestational, conceptual, and spiritual. Masculine is assertive, action-oriented, physical, and material. When in balance, beautiful and powerful creations are born. When out of balance, depression and sometimes even war ensue.

Located at the root or genital area. 1st Chakra.

7 KEYS & THE CHAKRAS

Key #1, Oneness
Located above the head. 7th Chakra.

Key #2, Inter-Dimension
Located between the eyes (third eye). 6th Chakra.

Key #3, Movement
Located at the throat (voice box). 5th Chakra.

Key #4, Paradox
Located above the heart. 4th Chakra.

Key #5, Exchange
Located above the solar plexus. 3rd Chakra.

Key #6, Personal Power
Located above the abdomen. 2nd Chakra.

Key #7, Yin~Yang
Located at the root or genital area. 1st Chakra.

SUCCESS STORIES

The following case studies assure you that the process works! And this format keeps us from sharing confidential information.

THE LESSON
Do it Your Way

A frustrated employee turned budding entrepreneur discovered her true path.

This client came to me knowing that things weren't right at work. She'd known this for awhile. She wanted guidance. In pattern interruption the image she pulled was of her on the beach talking with Jesus. (This image is always the perfect one for you, chosen by you, in the perfect time to answer your intended result.) His words, according to what she saw were, "You go back and do what you need to do. I am with you. I've done this my way, you do it your way." I watched her progress from afar. After this experience, she had the courage to start her business. It is gradually growing—her way. It's a great gift to the world, and a great gift from her heart. The image she held in her mind's eye that day gave her strength, courage and insight to boldly proceed in the direction of her dreams.

THE LESSON

The Power of Saying, "No"

A very powerful educated attorney had a vision, yet didn't know what to do about it.

My trademarked seven-step TurboCoaching program showed us that the step involving personal power was out of balance. Once this client got clear on his vision for his company, he was able to make requests with urgency. This got him an audience with a major U.S. corporate CEO which led to a future relationship with that corporate leader. Two months was all he needed. His life and his work were transformed, and his vision came to life.

THE LESSON

Don't Ignore the Shadow Side

Yet another study involved a public relations professional.

Her life was grounded in involvement with people. She knew her professional life was in good shape; yet her personal relationships would falter. She chose pattern interruption and discovered a subconscious stumbling block. The image in her subconscious was of her dad. During the session she pulled an image showing that she adored him, and then, she saw a dark side that she had never consciously acknowledged. Through the interpretation session she was able to see that she denied the shadow side in any of her relationships. Once she was aware of this pattern of denial, she was able to create relationships with people which were authentic, embracing both the lighter and darker sides of their personalities. When those sides were extreme, she could walk away without harm.